THE MOONLIT POND

九龍瀑

仙漱氣似清秋千尺長虹立
不流却有圓形通不底銀河倒勢
渴雲歇雨戰光雞窄白雷
喧響走收閒送九龍藏窟宅一淵
疑黯使人怯

白邨李炳浩

("Nine-Dragon Falls," Yi Byŏng-ho)

The Moonlit Pond

KOREAN CLASSICAL POEMS IN CHINESE

TRANSLATED & INTRODUCED BY

Sung-Il Lee

COPPER CANYON PRESS

Publication of this book is supported by a grant from the Korean Culture and Arts Foundation, the National Endowment for the Arts, and a grant from the Lannan Foundation. Additional support to Copper Canyon Press has been provided by the Washington State Arts Commission. Copper Canyon Press is in residence with Centrum at Fort Worden State Park.

ACKNOWLEDGMENTS: Special thanks are due to the Korean Culture and Arts Foundation for a grant which helped make this book possible.

Library of Congress Cataloging-in-Publication Data

The moonlit pond: Korean classical poems in Chinese / translated and introduced by Sung-Il Lee
p. cm.
ISBN 1-55659-076-8 (pbk.)
1. Chinese poetry – Korea – Translations into English. 2. Korean poetry – To 1900 – Translations into English. I. Lee, Sung-Il, 1943–
PL3064.5.E5M66 1997   97-21179

COPPER CANYON PRESS

P.O. BOX 271, PORT TOWNSEND, WASHINGTON 98368

To the Memory of
My Revered Grandfather,
Poet Yi Byong-ho (1870–1943)

Contents

PREFACE

THE IDEA OF TRANSLATING Korean poetry written in classical Chinese into English had been on my mind for a long time. I was not, however, able to carry this out until a few years ago, shortly after my English-language publication of four major modern Korean poets in a volume entitled *The Wind and the Waves* (Berkeley: Asian Humanities Press, 1989). This last project reawakened me to the truth that modern Korean poetry, although composed in the vernacular and often in free verse, has been greatly influenced by a long classical Chinese poetic tradition in Korea, which had been in the mainstream until the turn of the century. In theme, imagery, and diction, these modern poems reveal the feelings and rhythmic patterns found in classical Chinese poetry. I believe that a full understanding of modern Korean poetry is possible only when one has some familiarity with Korean classical poems in Chinese.

Born in the midtwentieth century, I belong to the generation of *Hangŭl*, the vernacular phonetic writing system. I grew up without much training in classical Chinese scholarship, but nonetheless undertook these translations in order to introduce this magnificent part of Korea's literary legacy to English readers.

The project has been challenging and precarious. Often, I was amazed at my own daring, because my native tongue is neither Chinese nor English, and my knowledge of classical Chinese is rudimentary. But, as a translator, I felt a great deal of gratification, while attempting to build a bridge between two poetic traditions separated by a deep chasm of linguistic differences.

The work has come to fruition with the help of Dr. Song

Joon-ho, Professor of Korean Classical Literature at Yonsei University. Professor Song, an expert in Korean classical poetry in Chinese, has been a genuine supporter of this project, and has given me a great deal of encouragement. I shall always cherish the memory of the many hours spent with him in pursuit of these poems.

I am also grateful to Mr. Sam Hamill, Editor of Copper Canyon Press, for agreeing to publish this work. A poet and translator of classical Chinese poetry, Mr. Hamill kindly took the trouble of going through my manuscript. I appreciate his suggestions, which have helped me to gear the work to contemporary American English.

I dedicate this slim volume to the memory of my grandfather, the late Yi Byŏng-ho, a renowned poet in classical Chinese. While translating his lines into a language he would never have understood, I felt both sad and happy – sad for the distance between his world and mine, and happy to realize that the two worlds, after all, are not too far apart.

INTRODUCTION

HUN-MIN-JŎNG-ŬM, the Korean phonetic writing system which is now called *Hangŭl,* was invented by King Sejong the Great (1397–1450) and his court scholars, and was promulgated by royal order in the midfifteenth century. Prior to that the only means of written communication in Korea was Chinese. There had been an effort to adapt Chinese written characters to vernacular literary works as early as in the ancient Shilla period (57 BC–935 AD), and scholars had created *Idu,* a way of recording literary works by borrowing Chinese characters that were similar in sound or meaning to the vernacular. But even after the promulgation of *Hun-min-jŏng-ŭm,* most literati kept writing in Chinese. Among the educated people, especially the tradition-oriented intellectuals, mastery of written Chinese and a broad knowledge of Chinese classics continued to remain an ideal until the end of the Chosŏn Dynasty (1392–1910). Indeed, the word "learning" traditionally meant the depth of understanding one had of the Chinese classics and the ability to write in literary Chinese. For centuries, young men aspiring to become courtiers or to be assigned to high posts in the government had to take *kwagŏ,* the national examination administered to recruit government officials. They were tested on their abilities to demonstrate their learning and literary gifts.

The above may lead readers to think that the spiritual side of Korean culture was an extension of Chinese culture. This is true to a certain degree, but only to the extent that English or French culture, for example, is an offspring of Roman civilization. As much as Latin scholarship was a criterion of learning in Europe, such was the case of scholarship in classical Chinese in Korea, although many magnificent literary works were still composed in the vernacular.

The history of Korean poetry in classical Chinese goes as far back as the ancient Three-Kingdom Period (18 BC-660 AD), and perhaps even farther. In fact, the oldest extant text of a lyric composed in Chinese belongs to the early part of the first century. But most scholars agree that Korean poetry in Chinese attained a high level, both in quality and quantity, in the late eighth century when the Unified Shilla Kingdom had built strong cultural ties with China, then under the reign of the T'ang Dynasty. Since then, poetry writing in classical Chinese never declined in Korea until the end of the Chosŏn Dynasty, after the turn of this century. Modern Korean literature, although written in the vernacular, cannot be completely separated from the long tradition of classical Chinese influence.

Although arranged in chronological order, the poems in this volume are not meant to provide a thorough historical overview. The book is rather a personal anthology, reflecting my own tastes. Certain themes recur, and readers may think that there were established literary conventions. Writers naturally like to see their lines echo the works of their predecessors, and thus, in time, an inherited literary tone becomes a convention. I would hope that this anthology is a treasury that reveals a great deal of diversity in theme, mood, and occasion. A detailed historical introduction about Korean classical poems in Chinese would not be in line with the spirit of this book. Following are some notes on the themes gleaned while I was translating them.

The transitoriness of life, along with a sense of futility about what one can accomplish in a lifetime, is a major theme which recurs in these poems. This concept of life as no more than a fleeting dream may go as far back as Chuang Tzu, whose parable of the dream of a butterfly expresses the insubstantiality of earthly existence. Life is a fleeting dream, to be followed by another dream that will last forever:

> The frosted moon shines cold on Swallow Pavilion.
> My friend is gone in a long, weary dream.
> Those who remain have ceased to grumble on growing old;
> Beauties who would entertain them now wear white hair.

As life is transitory, so is all the glory and pomp of a kingdom. Standing on the ruins of time, a poet contemplates the grandeur of the past, now fallen into decay. However, while immersed in these thoughts, he also attains the vision which enables him to see the present in the context of the flow of time:

> Passing by Yŏngmyŏng Temple the other day,
> I ascended to Pu-byŏk Pavilion.
> The moon was floating above the castle ruin,
> Clouds encircled the moss-grown steps.
> The legendary stallion is gone forever.
> Where are the successive monarchs loitering now?
> I sigh, standing on the windswept stair –
> The mountains are still green, and the river continues
>   to flow.

The notion of the transience of earthly glory has often led to pessimistic world-views or even to a brooding sense of doom, as in Old English poetry. A nation that has experienced the rise and fall of numerous kingdoms, Korea has given birth to many poets who wrote in the vein of *contemptus mundi*:

When the sun sets, the sky is inky-dark;
Deep in the mountains, the ravine is cloudy.
All the human wishes retained for a thousand years
Are finally fulfilled by a single mound.

This awareness of the transience of life and of worldly glory is manifested in many of these poems. However, Koreans, by nature, are an optimistic and pleasure-seeking people, keen on the enjoyment of life in the here-and-now. The following poem, before it was put into Chinese, was originally a folk song eulogizing the bliss of being alive, but with an undercurrent of the awareness of mortality:

Upon the thick ice of midwinter
Let us spread the frosted bamboo leaves.
Though I freeze to death with you,
I wish the cock would never crow.

The theme of *carpe diem* is explicitly presented in this poem; in translating a folk song, the poet recaptured the colloquial expressions of the original. In most classical poetry in Chinese, however, this theme was suppressed, as the Confucian ethic, which demanded asceticism as its moral principle, controlled the lives of Koreans for many centuries. Poems about the joys of simple life are plentiful in this collection, and the authors exult in the rewards of finding pleasure and peace of mind in a humble life.

As in *shijo* and *kasa*, two major poetic subgenres in the vernacular, an important theme in classical poetry in Chinese is the peace of mind derived from a simple life in nature, away from the worldly bustle, along with the gratification that comes to those who overcome worldly desires for fame and wealth. Ancient Taoism had significant influence on these poets:

Living alone in leisure in a hut by a stream,
I enjoy more than my share of moon and wind.
Though no one comes to visit, birds sing to me.
I move my cot near the bamboo grove, and lie down
　　to read.

Or:

Living alone in leisure where no one comes to visit,
I rejoice only at the moon shining on my solitary hut.
Do not ask, friend, what I wish to make of my life:
An endless wave of fog spreads far over mountain peaks.

The Confucian ethic, with its austere moral principles, advocated the suppression of "vulgar" desires inherent in human nature. The goal of spiritual aristocracy for a true man of integrity and learning was to find contentment in a life of penury and physical hardship. Thus, even with the possession of physical comfort and luxury, one might feel a deep sense of shame for not having transcended worldly pleasures.

Among the moral principles a man of integrity was to follow, loyalty to a monarch was supreme, and had to be maintained, even in the face of death. Over the centuries, many courtiers and scholars chose either death or seclusion when a new dynasty took power. Thus, when the boy king Tanjong, the sixth monarch of the Chosŏn Dynasty, was deposed by his uncle, several court scholars refused to serve the new king, and were executed for their plan to reinstate the deposed boy king. Following is the

valedictory poem by one of them, presumably composed at the
execution site:

Beating drums call for my life;
As I turn westward, the sun is about to set.
On the way to the netherworld there is no inn;
Where shall I find a lodge tonight?

The poise and calm with which the poet faces death while
wholeheartedly accepting the consequence of his moral choice is
displayed at that sublime moment which concludes his life.

Loyalty, however, often went further than patriotism. While
many poems were written about one's relationship to his king,
many others were written about longing for the beloved. The be-
loved might be the country or the king, but it also might be a par-
ent, friend, or lover. These poems of longing have a common
theme of constancy, where neither distance nor time can dimin-
ish love, but rather increases it. A courtier of the mid-Chosŏn
Dynasty, who opposed making a humiliating truce with the in-
vading Ching army, was taken to China as a prisoner at the close
of the war. He wrote this poem to his wife:

Though our conjugal love still deepens,
Our happiness lasted less than two years.
Now we are ten thousand miles from each other,
Our pledge of a hundred years together has proven vain.
The width of the land is hard for a letter to cross;
The breadth of the sky delays my journey even in dreams.
Now I cannot be sure of my safe return,
I bid you to raise well our unborn child.

Even at the Chinese court he refused to stoop and admit his "guilt" of high treason to the Chinese emperor, and was executed. The poet foresaw his death, and in his will to his wife he reconfirmed his unchanging love, while making it clear that he believed in the cause for which he would lose his life.

The Chosŏn Dynasty period gave birth to many women poets. In Confucian society, women were rarely granted the privilege of receiving a formal education. However, many gifted women taught themselves, attaining a high level of scholarship, and they wrote remarkable poems. There were two groups of these women writers – those who were born in upper-class families, and those who belonged to the lower strata of society, such as concubines or *kisaeng*, the Korean counterpart of the Japanese geisha. A *kisaeng* was a woman whose profession was to entertain people at gatherings, either formal or informal, with her skill in various arts, such as singing, playing musical instruments, dancing, and even composing poems. Inasmuch as her profession required a high level of mastery in several arts, the term *kisaeng* should be differentiated from the usual concept of a woman who sells herself merely for money; although a *kisaeng* was still considered to belong to a lower stratum in society.

In a typically Confucian society, romantic passion, though not an absolute taboo, was not a popular subject for poems. Even so, many women of letters, especially the concubines and the *kisaeng*, who were relatively free from the oppressive social ethos, wrote poems of longing, but the longing expressed is more about fidelity and constancy than erotic passion. Societal prejudice against these lower-class women may have motivated them to assert their dignity by remaining faithful to their loved ones:

Cold-stricken geese cry in the frost,
Crossing the mountain wall buried in silence.
I wake from a dream of my sweet love
To see the autumn moon brighten my window.

Or,

I am anxious to know how you are of late.
As moonbeams surge on the windowpanes, my longing
    deepens.
If footsteps in dreams can leave their traces,
The stony path near your home must be worn to sand.

Even among the works by these women, one does not expect
to find poems of seduction. Although society may have looked
down upon them, their poems reveal that, in spite of their
straightforward longing, they extolled the beauty of being true to
their precious ones, and to the spirit of fidelity. The feminine
touches are not the real essence of their poetry. Hidden under
the voices of longing and complaint, one finds the moral sinew
underlying all Korean classical poetry. When poetry reaches its
heights, it becomes irrelevant to whether the poet is male or fe-
male. A poem composed by a *kisaeng*, Hwang Jini, is worthy of
a first-rate poet in any poetic tradition:

Silence reigns over an old temple by the ruined palace;
A tall tree in the setting sun makes an onlooker sad.
Chilly fog spreads – the lingering dreams of the monks;
On the broken pagoda, time-stacked layers of dust.
Where a royal bird would soar, nameless birds fly;
Where azaleas bloom no more, sheep and cattle graze.

The overlooking mountain may recall pomp and glory;
Did it know spring would turn quickly into autumn?

The poem is all the more poignant for the awareness that she is able to express about the transitoriness of life and the ephemerality of her physical beauty. Just as spring turns into autumn, so, she realizes, her life as a *kisaeng* will end when her youth is gone.

Korean poets writing in Chinese used not only the Chinese language, but the resources and conventions of classical Chinese poetry as well, including the use of the five- and seven-character line in quatrain or octave; syntactic parallelism; composition by couplet; the juxtaposition of imagery to convey sensibility and plurisignation. Korean poets also liked to model famous Chinese classics. Yet despite apparent similarities which echo classical Chinese poetry in form and content, Korean classical poetry in Chinese has its own unique tradition.

These observations on Korean classical poetry in Chinese are by no means comprehensive. In this brief sketch, I have attempted to introduce to the reader a small part of the grand panorama that unfolds as we turn from one poem to another in a tradition spanning more than a millennium.

THE MOONLIT POND

On a Rainy Autumn Night

CH'OE CH'I-WŎN (857–?)

The autumn wind breeds only mournful songs,
Though few in the world would know my mind.
Outside the window, midnight rain still drizzles
As I sit before a lamp, thoughts rushing far away.

At His Hermitage on Mount Kaya

CH'OE CH'I-WŎN (857–?)

The roaring rush over rocks echoes to the peaks,
Drowning human voices coming from nearby.
Fearing that the noise of arguing might burn my ears,
I taught the stream to deafen even mountains.

From the Mirror Peak

CH'OE CH'I-WŎN (857-?)

Fog-encircled peaks overlook the flowing river.
The village sits in a mirror, facing the green mountain.
A lone boat from somewhere drifts away with a full-blown sail,
Like a bird that flies away, leaving no trace.

Ch'oe Ch'i-won, a scholar-poet of the late Shilla Kingdom, went to China in
868, and became a courtier after passing the T'ang civil service examination.
He returned to his homeland to serve at the court, but, disillusioned with the
corruption of the high society, spent his last years at a hermitage on Mount
Kaya.

Cold Pine Pavilion

CHANG YŎN-U (?–1015)

The moon is bright over Cold Pine Pavilion;
The autumn waves are calm on Mirror Lake.
Crying, a seagull flies away only to return;
That bird over the sand must have a message for me.

Chang Yŏn-u was a high-ranking courtier of the Koryŏ Dynasty.

A Quatrain

CH'OE HANG (?-1024)

The moonbeam overflowing the yard is a smokeless candle;
The mountain shadow that has stolen into my room is an
    unbidden guest.
Pines are my lyre that the wind plays without notes;
Alone, I exult in the music, though I cannot share it with others.

Ch'oe Hang was a high-ranking courtier of the Koryŏ Dynasty, much respected
for his integrity and uprightness.

The Taedong River

CHŎNG CHI-SANG (?–1135)

As the rain stops, the long bank looks greener.
Seeing you off on a ferry moves me to a sad song.
When will the Taedong River dry up and cease to flow?
Farewell tears add yearly to the green ripples.

Bidding Farewell

CHŎNG CHI-SANG (?–1135)

A single leaf falls in the yard.
Near my desk, crickets chirp sadly.
I know I cannot hold you here.
I wonder where your journey will take you.
My longing will follow you to where the mountains end,
As I seek you in my dream on a moonlit night.
When the spring river ripples green along the bank,
I beg you not to forget your promise to return.

Chŏng Chi-san was a poet-scholar-courtier of the Koryŏ Dynasty. He was
falsely accused of high treason by his political rivals and was executed.

The Pinks

CHŎNG SŬP-MYŎNG (?–1151)

The whole world loves the beauty of peonies;
People plant and grow them to adorn their gardens.
Yet who will know that in the grass-entangled field
Lovely patches of flowers, though untended, still grow?
Their tints are cast on the pond like moonbeams;
Their fragrance spreads in the wind from hilltop trees.
As noblemen rarely visit this remote deserted valley,
The pinks reveal their beauty only to the old ploughman.

Chŏng Sŭp-myŏng was a courtier of the Koryŏ Dynasty.

Mountain Hermitage After a Rainy Night

KO CHO-GI (?–1157)

Rain fell last night on my pine-encircled cot,
And the waterfall sounds louder over my pillow.
At dawn I look on the tree in the yard;
The birds have not yet awakened to leave their nest.

Ko Cho-gi was a courtier of the Koryŏ Dynasty.

After a Slumber

CH'OE YU-CH'ŎNG (1095–1174)

The spring grass has already turned green;
Butterflies flutter, flocking in the yard.
The east wind robs me of sweet slumber,
Blowing on my bed, lifting my garment.
I awake to find that only silence reigns,
While late sunrays fall on the trees.
About to utter a word in wonder, leaning on the railing,
I lose my discerning mind in tranquil quietude.

Ch'oe Yu-ch'ŏng was a courtier of the Koryŏ Dynasty.

Mountain Cottage

Yi In-ro (1152–1220)

Though spring is gone, flowers still bloom;
Though the sky is clear, the ravine is dark.
The nightingale's song, heard in broad daylight,
Reminds me – home is deep in the mountains.

Night Rain on the Sosang River

YI IN-RO (1152–1220)

A surge of blue waves spreads autumn on the shore;
Wind streaks thin rain on the returning boat.
As night comes, the boat is moored among riverside bamboos;
The rustle of the cold-stricken leaves deepens my sorrow.

To My Drinking Friend

YI IN-RO (1152–1220)

I can handle only a few bowls of wine,
While you can drink a whole barrel.
But when our inebriation reaches its height,
My ecstasy can very well rival yours.
The spring breeze blows on our warm cheeks
While our worries melt away in flowing cups.
What need for us to count the number
When each of us can have his fill?

Yi In-ro, a prominent scholar and poet of the Koryŏ Dynasty, held several high posts in the government. He liked to indulge in wine and poetry, and befriended many of the literati.

Along the Naktong River

YI KYU-BO (1168–1241)

Having trod the winding path through mountains,
I now step leisurely along the Naktong River.
Where the grass is rich, dewdrops glitter.
Wind stopped blowing through tranquil pines.
The autumn river ripples green as a swimming duck's head,
And fog at sunrise is dyed crimson.
Who will know that the weary wayfarer
Is a poet whose lines have swept the world?

Visiting a Temple on a Spring Day

YI KYU-BO (1168–1241)

In gentle breeze and warm sun, birds sing merrily;
In the shade of drooping willows, the temple gate is half closed.
While fallen petals cover the earth, the drunken monk sleeps.
The air of peace and calm lingers in his mountain hermitage.

The Moon in the Well

YI KYU-BO (1168–1241)

A monk grew enamored of the moon in a well,
So he drew moonlit water to pour in a jar.
When he came back to the temple, he found,
As he tilted the jar, the moon was gone.

Yi Kyu-bo was a scholar, poet, and government official of the Koryŏ Dynasty.
He is famous for having once persuaded invading Mongolian troops to retreat
through the power of a single letter.

Spring Sentiment

CHIN HWA (12TH–13TH CENTURY)

While plum blossoms wilt and willows flow down,
My leisurely steps in the spring breeze grow slower.
Now the waterside tavern is closed and people's talk ceased,
Spring rain sweeps the river, threads of thin emerald.

Late Spring

CHIN HWA (12TH–13TH CENTURY)

Moss grows thick in the rain-soaked garden,
But my gate remains closed, since no one visits.
Fallen petals on the steps are an inch deep;
The east wind blows them away only to blow them back again.

Chin Hwa was a poet of the Koryŏ Dynasty.

The Swallow Pavilion

CHANG IL (1207–1276)

The frosty moon shines cold on Swallow Pavilion.
My friend is gone in a long, weary dream.
Those who remain have ceased to grumble on growing old;
Beauties who would entertain them now wear white hair.

Chang Il was a courtier and military commander of the Koryŏ Dynasty.

On a Spring Day

WANG PAEK (1277–1350)

After last night's fog soaked my thatched roof,
Peach blossoms near the bamboo are suddenly in full bloom.
Drunk with wine, I forget the snowy streaks of my hair –
I wear a flowery crown, standing in the spring breeze.

Wang Paek, a descendent of the royal family of the Shilla Dynasty, was a
courtier of the Koryŏ Dynasty.

A Touch of Grace

YI JE-HYŎN (1287–1367)

As I was washing silk by a willow-drawn stream,
A man riding a white horse held my hand, and took my heart.
Though rain drips from the eaves for three months,
How can his fragrance lingering on my fingers be washed away?

Yi Je-hyŏn was a poet, scholar, and courtier of the late Koryŏ Dynasty. He
translated several folk songs into Chinese, this poem being one of them.

Stepping off the Rain

YI GOK (1298–1351)

A mansion guarded by an elm stands by the road;
Its tall gate was built for prosperous posterity.
Now its dwellers have moved away, no cart comes by –
Only the passersby step in to avoid the rain.

Yi Gok, a courtier, scholar, and diplomat of the Koryŏ Dynasty, was the father
of Yi Saek, whose works appear later in this volume.

Sewing for Her Husband

SŎL SON (?-1360)

The bright moon that lights the sky above
Casts beams into this long autumn night.
A sad wind blows from the northwest,
And crickets chirp near my bed.
You, love, are far away on a mission,
And I keep this empty room alone.
What pains me most is not my being alone in this room –
I worry that you won't have enough to wear.

Sŏl Son, a man of Uigur descent, served the Mongolian dynasty of China for
some time, but later became a naturalized Korean and was granted land and
titles.

From a Flunky to a Success

YI KONG-SU (1308–1366)

When names in gold glitter in the sun,
A shady hut breeds youthful ambition.
Who in the cold bleak palace of the moon will know
A laurel branch is still waiting to be plucked?

Yi Kong-su was a courtier and diplomat of the late Koryŏ Dynasty.

Admonition

NA-ONG (1320–1376)

While I desperately pursued glory in the dusty world,
How could I know that frost would settle on my hair?
Desire for glory burns people like hell-fire;
How many since bygone days have perished in its flame?

Na-ong was a famous Buddhist monk who lived during the latter years of the
Koryŏ Dynasty.

A Drunken Song

YI DAL-CH'UNG (?–1385)

When I wish to wash my feet,
Will the clear stream take in my dirt?
When I wish to wash my ears,
Will the clear brook swallow my shame?
A cripple by birth as I am,
I won't be laughed at if I never stir abroad.
Stone-deaf by birth as I am,
I won't be ridiculed for not hearing rough words.
"To be of no use can be of great use sometimes."
I shall repeat the words three times each day.

Yi Dal-ch'ung was a scholar, poet, and high-ranking government official
toward the end of the Koryŏ Dynasty. The quotation is from the first chapter
of *Chuang Tzu*.

An Improvisation

YI SAEK (1328–1396)

The joy of living in seclusion deepens as I grow older,
For a new poem is born wherever I turn my eyes.
Flowers that withstood the wind fall of their own accord;
Thin rain left by clouds has not yet cleared.
The frail butterfly over the fence has left the twig where it sat,
And the silken dove has flown from the eave to sing in the
    woods.
To attain a vision transcending the here and now is not my
    concern:
What I see is much too clear, as in a mirror.

At Pu-byŏk Pavilion

YI SAEK (1328–1396)

Passing by Yŏngmyŏng Temple the other day,
I ascended to Pu-byŏk Pavilion.
The moon was floating above the castle ruin,
Clouds encircled the moss-grown steps.
The legendary stallion is gone forever.
Where are the successive monarchs loitering now?
I sigh, standing on the windswept stair –
The mountains are still green, and the river continues to flow.

In Late Spring

YI SAEK (1328–1396)

Grass becomes greener in the south while spring lingers.
Birds call one another in the quiet yard.
Under a sky threatening rain, mountains darken.
Now the petals have fallen, lingering winds sweep the yard.
How many years have I wielded my writing brush without fear?
When shall I resign my post and head for the carefree stream?
Since olden days, big-hearted men have taken the world lightly;
A mere follower of petty learning, I feel sorry for my small self.

Yi Saek, a prominent scholar toward the end of the Koryŏ Dynasty, held several high posts in the government. He was one of the great thinkers of his age, along with Chŏng Mong-ju, Kil Jae, and Yi Sung-in.

An Improvisation

CHO UN-HŬL (1332–1404)

Only at noon I tell my boy to open the brushwood gate.
I step out of my woodland cottage to sit on a mossy rock.
Last night in the mountains, the wind and rain were fierce;
Many a petal comes drifting down the stream.

Cho Un-hŭl, a man of letters toward the end of the Koryŏ Dynasty, served
both the Koryŏ and the Chosŏn dynasties. Later he withdrew from public life
and lived in seclusion. This poem probably alludes to political turmoil.

Spring Sentiment

CHŎNG MONG-JU (1337–1392)

Thin spring rain, barely audible,
Grows louder as the night deepens.
When snow melts into the growing stream,
Many a sprout prepares to burst out.

At Myŏng-wŏn Pavilion

CHŎNG MONG-JU (1337–1392)

The clear stream flows, circling the rocky wall;
The new pavilion commands a wide view.
Clouds above the southern field are tinged with gold;
From the western hill, cool breezes announce morning.
A lord with grace should have two thousand bushels at his
    disposal,
And drink three hundred bowls of wine with his long-missed
    friend.
Unable to suppress the wish to blow a jade flute deep into night,
I stroll with the bright moon ascending the sky.

Chŏng Mong-ju, a prominent scholar and courtier of the late Koryŏ Dynasty,
remained loyal to the declining monarchy, and was killed by Yi Pang-won, who
later became the third monarch of the Chosŏn Dynasty.

On the First of April

CHŎNG DO-JŎN (1337–1398)

Mountain birds have stopped singing; fallen petals drift.
When I am still away from home, spring already fades.
A sudden rise of the south wind awakens my longing,
And blows on my grassy yard overflowing with green.

Visiting a Recluse

Chŏng Do-jŏn (1337–1398)

As autumn clouds spread far over the mountains,
Leaves fall quietly to cover the earth in crimson.
I stop my horse at a bridge to ask my way back,
Unaware that I have stepped into a picture.

Chŏng Do-jŏn, a courtier in the reign of the last kings of the Koryŏ Dynasty,
helped Yi Sŏng-gye to start a new monarchy, the Chosŏn Dynasty.

On a Swift Boat

KIM KU-YONG (1338–1384)

From the swift boat with a full-blown sail
Mountains pass quickly, shoreline gliding by.
In a foreign land, one asks about custom;
But beautiful scenery compels me to compose lines.
On a stretch of land where ancient kingdoms prospered,
The month of May flows on the crystal stream.
Do not regret that you have neither wealth nor fame;
Don't wind and moon follow wherever you go?

Kim Ku-yong, a courtier toward the end of the Koryŏ Dynasty, went to China
on a diplomatic mission, and died there of illness.

To My Silent Teacher

KIM JE-AN (?-1368)

Worldly affairs lead to endless debates on right and wrong;
Ten-years' sojourn in the mud has only stained my robes.
In the spring breeze, flowers wilt and birds sing.
Where do you live in the mountains with your gate firmly
closed?

Kim Je-an, Kim Ku-yong's younger brother, was also a courtier toward the
end of the Koryŏ Dynasty. After returning from a trip to China on a diplomatic
mission, he became a victim of political intrigue and was killed.

The New-Fallen Snow

YI SUNG-IN (1349–1392)

When the sky at the year's end stretches far,
New-fallen snow covers mountains and rivers.
Birds have lost their nests in mountain trees.
The monk looks for a rivulet flowing over rocks.
When starving crows caw above the field,
Frozen willows lean along the stream.
As I wonder where a village sits,
Far from the forest, white smoke rises.

Mountain Hermitage

YI SUNG-IN (1349–1392)

Where the mountain path branches north and south,
Rain-soaked pine pollen drifts to cover the earth.
As the hermit returns to his hut with water from the well,
A stream of blue smoke rises to dye white clouds.

Yi Sung-in, one of the most prominent men of letters toward the end of the
Koryŏ Dynnasty, was an expert in international relationships and was a
distinguished diplomat. When the Chosŏn Dynasty was founded, he was killed
by an assassin sent by Chŏng Do-jŏn, who had betrayed the old monarchy.

On a Spring Day

KWŎN KŬN (1352–1409)

A sudden blow of the spring breeze brings the bright season
     nearer,
But the thin, windblown rain does not clear up till late.
Around the corner of the house, an apricot is ready to bloom;
A few dew-laden branches lean toward me as I look on.

Kwŏn Kŭn, a courtier-scholar who served the last monarchs of the Koryŏ
Dynasty, also held high offices in the reign of the first three kings of the Chosŏn
Dynasty.

Life in Leisure

Living alone in leisure in a hut by a stream,
I enjoy more than my share of moon and wind.
Though no one comes to visit, birds sing to me.
I move my cot near the bamboo grove, and lie down to read.

Kil Jae, a student of Yi Saek and Chŏng Mong-ju, was a prominent scholar-educator. When he was assigned to a high post in the government of the newly founded Chosŏn Dynasty, he declined the offer, saying that he could not serve two monarchies. He lived the remainder of his life in seclusion, teaching young men – several of whom became noted scholars in their own right – until his death.

After an Old Song

Upon the thick ice of midwinter
Let us spread the frosted bamboo leaves.
Though I freeze to death with you,
I wish the cock would never crow.

Upon Looking at a Landscape

KIM SU-ON (1409–1481)

The exquisite drawing reveals a divine art,
With all the grass and flowers shining in spring light.
But all this, after all, is a scene of illusion;
Who will know both the picture and I are but fleeting shadows?

Kim Su-on, a man of great learning, contributed immensely to the develop-
ment of writing in the vernacular by translating many classics, including
Buddhist scriptures.

Before Execution

SŎNG SAM-MUN (1418–1456)

Beating drums call for my life;
As I turn westward, the sun is about to set.
On the way to the netherworld there is no inn;
Where shall I find a lodge tonight?

Sŏng Sam-mun was one of the court scholars who helped King Sejong the
Great invent *Hun-min-jŏng-ŭm*, the phonetic writing system in the vernacular.
When Prince Suyang usurped the throne by forcing the boy king Tanjong, his
nephew, to abdicate, Sŏng Sam-mun conspired with those loyal to the deposed
king to assassinate Prince Suyang and reinstate Tanjong. The plot was
divulged, and Sŏng Sam-mun, along with other conspirators, was executed.

Listening to a Nightingale

DEPOSED KING TANJONG
(1441–1457)

Driven out of the court to become a sorrowful bird,
The wandering soul casts its lonely shadow deep in the
    mountains.
Night after night, deprived of sleep, it longs in vain for rest;
Year after year, its deepening sorrow never reaches its bounds.
As its crying stops at dawn, the fading moon looks pale;
The stream of the spring ravine is dyed crimson by fallen petals.
When the sky is deaf to the blood-choked supplication,
Why should my grief-stricken soul have ears to listen?

Tanjong, the sixth monarch of the Chosŏn Dynasty, ascended the throne when
he was a child. His uncle, Prince Suyang, deposed him and, after ascending the
throne, exiled Tanjong to a remote mountainous region, where he was put to
death by the new king's order. The poem contains an allusion to the legend of a
king in ancient China who is said to have become a nightingale after expulsion
from his court.

Sitting Alone

I sit alone, with no visitors around,
As rain settles over the empty yard.
A fish stirs in the pond, shaking the lotus leaves;
A magpie alights on that branch, and it wavers.
Though damp, my lyre can still be strummed;
Though getting cold, my fire-pot still burns.
Since the road is muddy outside the house,
Why not keep my gate closed all day long?

Laughing at Myself

SŎ KŎ-JŎNG (1420–1488)

Having composed a poem, I compose another;
All day long I care about nothing but composing.
As I recall, I have so far composed ten thousand poems;
I know I shall stop composing only on my deathbed.

Sŏ Kŏ-jŏng, a scholar-poet-courtier, was one of the foremost men of letters
in the early part of the Chosŏn Dynasty.

After a Folk Song

SŎNG KAN (1427–1456)

Green bamboos remain upright in the wind;
But duckweed drifts on the wavering water.
I wish you to be like green bamboo
And not resemble duckweed, floating down the stream.

Sŏng Kan was a scholar-poet-courtier in the early part of the Chosŏn Dynasty.

Fallen Leaves

KIM SHI-SŬP (1435–1493)

Do not sweep the fallen leaves,
For they are pleasant to hear on clear nights.
In the wind, they rustle, as if sighing;
In the moonlight, their shadows flutter.
They knock on the window to wake a traveler;
Covering stairs, they hide moss.
Sad, the sight of them getting wet in rain;
Let them wither away deep in the mountains.

Kim Shi-sŭp became a monk when Prince Suyang usurped the throne after
forcing the boy king Tanjong to abdicate. He spent all his life writing books
and translating Buddhist scriptures.

North Expedition

NAM YI (1441–1468)

The rocks of Mount Paektu will whet my sword;
My horse will drink up Tuman River.
If a man of twenty is unable to bring peace to his land,
Who in later ages will call him a true-born man?

Nam Yi was a brilliant military leader, and he became the minister of national
defense when he was only twenty-six. Those who were envious of his success
conspired to use this poem to accuse him of harboring treasonous thoughts,
and he was executed by royal order.

An Old General

PAK WI-GYŎM

(MID-15TH CENTURY)

The white horse neighing in the wind is tied to a willow;
The general's sword remains in the sheath, for there is no war.
Before he has done his share, he has grown old;
In his dreams, he treads the mountainous front in deep snow.

Pak Wi-gyŏm was a military commander in the early part of the Chosŏn
Dynasty. After withdrawing from his military career, he lived the remainder
of his life in seclusion.

Looking at a Drawing of Red Plum Blossoms

CHO WI (1454–1503)

Waking up from a dream, I walk into the moonlit yard.
Plum blossom fragrance lingers where their shadows lie.
Indifferent to their inner jade-blue-white color,
Last night an east-wind gust dyed them in an evening glow.

Cho Wi was a prominent scholar-poet-courtier of the early
Chosŏn Dynasty.

Recluse Life

KIM KOENG-P'IL (1454–1504)

Living alone in leisure where no one comes to visit,
I rejoice only at the moon shining on my solitary hut.
Do not ask, friend, what I wish to make of my life:
An endless wave of fog spreads far over mountain peaks.

Kim Koeng-p'il, a prominent scholar-courtier of the early Chosŏn Dynasty,
took several high posts in the government. During the bloody purge of 1498, he
was forced into exile, and was later killed during the following purge of 1504.

The Pear-Blossom Pavilion

SHIN CHAM (1491–1554)

Thirty springs have passed since I first came here;
Visiting the site of my past pleasure only grieves my heart.
In the yard, the pear tree still blossoms,
But those who sang and danced are gone.

Shin Cham was a government official of the early Chosŏn Dynasty.

Elegy for Myself

KI JOON (1492–1521)

When the sun sets, the sky is inky dark;
Deep in the mountains, the ravine is cloudy.
All the human wishes retained for a thousand years
Are finally fulfilled by a single mound.

Ki Joon, a disciple of Cho Kwang-jo, the great scholar and political reformer
who was killed in a court intrigue, was himself a courtier who was forced into
exile, where he was eventually strangled to death by an assassin.

Falling-Petals Rock

HONG CH'UN-KYŎNG (1497–1548)

When the kingdom fell, mountains and streams looked different;
How many times has the moon over the river waxed and waned
  since then?
Around Falling-Petals Rock, flowers still bloom;
The stormy wind from that day has never died away.

Hong Ch'un-kyŏng was a courtier of the mid-Chosŏn Dynasty. On the day of
the fall of the Paekje Kingdom, hundreds of court ladies jumped into the White
Horse River from a rock known as "Falling-Petals Rock," preferring death to
the humiliation to be inflicted upon them by the invading soldiers of Shilla and
its ally, the Chinese T'ang.

Bidding Farewell to So Sĕyang

HWANG JINI (1506–1544)

Paulownia leaves fall on the moonlit yard;
In the frost, wild chrysanthemums turn yellow.
In the tall pavilion where the sky looks low,
We have lost count of the winecups we have emptied.
The stream flows cold, to the beat of my lyre;
Plum blossom fragrance mingles with the tune of his flute.
When we have bidden farewell tomorrow morning,
Our longing will flow on like an endless stream.

On Full-Moon Hill

HWANG JINI (1506–1544)

Silence reigns over an old temple by the ruined palace;
A tall tree in the setting sun makes an onlooker sad.
Chilly fog spreads – the lingering dreams of the monks;
On the broken pagoda, time-stacked layers of dust.
Where a royal bird would soar, nameless birds fly;
Where azaleas bloom no more, sheep and cattle graze.
The overlooking mountain may recall pomp and glory;
Did it know spring would turn quickly into autumn?

Meeting in Dreams

Pining for each other, we can meet only in dreams;
Yet while I rejoice to see you there, you rejoice to see me here.
If we are to dream of each other on a night to come,
Let us set out at the same time to meet on the road.

Hwang Jini, a famous female poet of the mid-Chosŏn Dynasty, was a *kisaeng*,
and in her time had romantic affairs with several men of distinction.

Looking Back

SHIM SU-KYŎNG (1516–1599)

Living in this world is like making drunken blunders –
Who will know what goals I harbored all these years?
Life and death, prosperity and misfortune, all depend on luck;
There is time for shame or glory, for worries or for joy.
Now I'm blessed with a long life, despite ill health,
I'm embarrassed to have held a minister's post.
Helping my king to rule was beyond my ability;
Too late, I learned my place was plowing fields.

At Jŏng-wŏn Pavilion

SHIM SU-KYŎNG (1516–1599)

I laugh at myself, making such a fuss of this fleeting life;
My unsettled life year after year has only added more white hair.
Who will know that the lone traveler sleeping behind the curtain
Is one who once lay in dazzling garments of silk?
When the moon is fair, a night away from home is slow;
Fallen petals in the yard tell me spring is passing.
Attaining glory is far from my life's goal;
Pursuing hollow fame, I have done wrong.

Shim Su-kyŏng was a courtier of the mid-Chosŏn Dynasty.

Visiting an Old Temple

CH'ŎNG-HŎ (1520–1604)

Flowers wilt, but the temple gate remains closed.
Spring deepens, but the awaited one does not return.
In the wind, a crane's shadow from its high nest:
A sailing cloud tinges the robe of a meditating monk.

Ch'ŏng-hŏ, a Buddhist monk, rallied an army of monks to fight the invading
Japanese when the Seven-Year War started in 1592, although he was over
seventy years old.

The Full Moon

Song Ik-p'il (1534–1599)

The crescent moon complains that it waxes so slowly;
How is it that once full, it wanes so quickly?
Of the thirty nights, it can remain full only one –
Whatever pertains to human life, after all, is the same.

White-Horse River

SONG IK-P'IL (1534–1599)

The old kingdom's prosperity has all turned into a dune,
Laughter-filled banquets hushed by a nightingale's song.
Peacefully quiet, a cloud crosses over a hill;
Bearing no trace of the fallen petals, the river flows on.
A white-haired ferryman weeps, remembering old days,
When a flute sounded over autumn hills.
Where are the souls of loyal subjects resting now?
One may as well dream of idling on a boat in the Five Lakes.

This poem alludes to the same incident as that in the poem "Falling-Petals
Rock" by Hong Chŭn-kyong.

Riding in the Wood

SONG IK-P'IL (1534–1599)

Riding in the wood, I forget to rest; resting, I forget to ride on.
Letting my horse rest in the shade, I listen to the water.
How many after me, as before me, will ride on this same road?
We all must turn into nothing; why, then, must we fight?

Song Ik-p'il was a scholar of the mid-Chosŏn Dynasty. Because he was born
out of wedlock, he could not hold public office, though educated many youths
who later became great scholars.

Flower-Rock Pavilion

Yi Yi (1536–1584)

Autumn deepens over the woodland pavilion;
The sentiment of an exile knows no bounds.
The far stretch of water joins the blue sky;
Red leaves burn in the setting sun.
The mountain lifts the floating moon;
Above the stream, the distant wind remains.
Where do cold-stricken wild geese all go?
Their crying fades into darkening clouds.

Yi Yi, a great scholar of the mid-Chosŏn Dynasty, was one of the two pillars of Neo-Confucian thinking, the other being the renowned Yi Hwang. Yi Yi was an infant prodigy who was able to compose poems in Chinese by the age of seven.

A Night at the Temple

CHŎNG CH'ŎL (1536–1593)

The rustle of falling windblown leaves
I took for the sound of sparse rain.
I asked a monk to go out and see if it was raining;
He came back to say the moon was hung high on a bough.

Rainy Night

CHŎNG CHʼŎL (1536–1593)

Cold night rain rustles the bamboo,
And crickets tell of autumn near my bed.
How can I hold the fleeting years at bay?
I cannot keep my hair from turning white.

A Pensive Moment

CHŎNG CH'ŎL (1536–1593)

Over the court wall, trees are dense on the hill;
In my dreams, I return to climb palace stairs.
A night bird's shrill cry splits the mountain bamboo:
That is when a lonely subject's hair turns white.

Chŏng Ch'ŏl, whose pen name was Song-gang, was a prominent scholar-poet-courtier-musician of the mid-Chosŏn Dynasty, and was a master of *kasa*, long prose-poetry in the vernacular. He was forced into exile on several occasions due to his political affiliations and finally died on Kanghwa Island. "A Pensive Moment" presumably refers to one of these times of exile.

Hong-kyŏng Temple

PAEK KWANG-HUN (1537–1582)

Autumn grass surrounds the bygone kingdom's temple;
On a crumbling stone the engraved lines fade.
A thousand years lie hidden in the flowing stream;
In the sunset, I watch returning clouds.

Life in Leisure

PAEK KWANG-HUN (1537–1582)

When I was about to think spring was coming,
Last night's rain had already swept the gateway.
Leisurely clouds cast their shadows across the peaks;
Birds warble pleasing notes in the trees.
I walk to the stream to sit on the bank,
And return through flowers, still dreaming.
I feel like tasting fresh-brewed wine.
My aging wife already knows, and brings it.

Paek Kwang-hun was a poet and calligrapher of the mid-Chosŏn Dynasty.

A Song on Chestnuts

YI SAN-HAE (1538–1609)

Three sons are born of a single paunch;
And the middle one has two flat sides.
When autumn comes, the chestnuts fall one after another;
It is hard to tell which is older, which younger.

Yi San-hae, a descendent of Yi Saek, was a high-ranking courtier of the mid-
Chosŏn Dynasty.

A Temple in the Mountains

Yi Dal (1539–1612)

The temple is buried in white clouds;
But the monk does not sweep them away.
As he opens the gate to receive a guest,
All the vales look hazy with flying pine pollen.

A Song of Sunset

YI DAL (1539–1612)

As sunset glow spreads on the west bank of the lake,
Those who befriended flowers are wary of drunken steps.
As they stagger on the road to the pleasure quarters,
From every window, the tune of irresistible charm.

An Abortive Harvest

Yi Dal (1539–1612)

A neighbor boy comes to collect jujubes;
The old man rushes out to catch the thief.
Running away, the boy turns to yell:
"You shouldn't live till jujubes ripen next year!"

Yi Dal was a prominent poet of the mid-Chosŏn Dynasty.

Hansan Isle at Night

ADMIRAL YI SUN-SHIN (1545–1598)

As autumn rays darken over the sea,
Cold, surprised geese flock high in the sky.
As I keep turning through the sleepless night,
Fading moonbeams fall on my bow and sword.

Yi Sun-shin is a legendary and revered figure in Korean history. A peerless
admiral, he invented the ironclad battleship (the "turtle boat") and saved
the nation by leading the navy in the Seven-Year War against the invading
Japanese.

To Kyerang

YU HI-KYŎNG (1545–1636)

Once I bade you farewell, clouds came between us;
Unable to suppress my longing, I keep turning in my bed.
The postal bird does not come to bring news from you;
I can hardly bear hearing rain on paulownia leaves.

Lamenting Kyerang's Death

YU HI-KYŎNG (1545–1636)

My girl, with bright eyes, snowy teeth, and raised brow,
Now you have followed the floating clouds, but to where?
Now your lovely soul has left for the netherworld,
Who will bury your jade bones in your home soil?

Yu Hi-kyŏng, a scholar of the mid-Chosŏn Dynasty, rallied an army of
civilians to fight the invading Japanese when the Seven-Year War started in
1592. "Kyerang" is Yi Mae-ch'ang, whose works appear later in this volume.

Silent Farewell

Im Je (1549–1587)

A girl of fifteen crossed the crystal-clear stream,
Yet shyness kept her tongue-tied in his presence.
When she came home, she firmly closed her door,
And silently wept to see the moon on a pear bough.

On Taedong River

Im Je (1549–1587)

As I watch girls walking on spring grass,
Willows drooping on the river make my heart ache.
If I could weave these thread-like willows,
I'd make a gown in which my love could dance.

A Song of Taedong River

Im Je (1549–1587)

Lovers bidding farewell break willow branches,
Though the broken boughs cannot hold the leaving.
Mixed with tears lovely girls have shed,
The fog-laden stream glitters sadly in the setting sun.

Im Je, a poet of the mid-Chosŏn Dynasty, was reputed to have been a man
of phenomenal memory, supposedly memorizing a thousand words of verse
per day. He was a noted scholar who stressed the importance of a Korea
more independent of China. He eventually left the court to live in subrural
surroundings.

A Love Song

HŎ NANSŎLHŎN (1563–1589)

On the calm autumn pond, jade-blue ripples glitter;
She moors her boat where lotus flowers bloom.
Seeing her love across the water, she throws a lotus seed,
And blushes for half a day, worrying that others may have seen.

Hŏ Nansŏlhŏn was one of the great writers of the Chosŏn Dynasty. Her sister
Hŏ Kyun was the author of the first novel written in Korean.

Waiting

Yi Ok-bong (?-1592)

Having promised to come, why are you so late?
Plum blossoms in the yard are ready to wilt.
A sudden cawing of a magpie on the branch
Makes me line my eyebrows, looking into an empty mirror.

The cawing of a magpie, according to Korean folklore, announces the coming
of a long-awaited person.

To Un-gang

YI OK-BONG (?–1592)

I am anxious to know how you are of late.
As moonbeams surge on the windowpanes, my longing deepens.
If footsteps in dreams can leave their traces,
The stony path near your home must be worn to sand.

After Bidding Farewell

Yi Ok-bong (?–1592)

Tonight, grief overruns my heart
As the moon sinks into wide waves.
I wonder where my beloved will sleep tonight:
Lying in his lodge, he will hear geese flocking far above.

Yi Ok-bong was a concubine.

On an Autumn Night

Sŭng Yi-kyo (16th century)

Cold-stricken geese cry in the frost,
Crossing the mountain wall buried in silence.
I wake from a dream of my sweet love
To see the autumn moon brighten my window.

Sŭng Yi-kyo was a *kisaeng*.

After Saying Farewell

Sŏ Yŏngsugak

(16TH–17TH CENTURY)

After seeing off my love when dusk fell on the mountain,
I returned to lie down where white clouds float above.
Against the old wall a lyre is leaning –
To be strummed by wind from the pines.

Sŏ Yŏngsugak, a well-born woman, was a prolific and celebrated poet.

Visiting a Monk in Seclusion

YI JONG-GUI (1564–1635)

Over the winding rocky path, my staff kept slipping on moss
While thin clouds floated over the wind-bells' ringing.
An attendant monk came out to greet me, and said
His mentor slept on the other mountain and hadn't yet returned.

Yi Jong-gui was a courtier-scholar of the mid-Chosŏn Dynasty.

Alone at Night

Kwŏn P'il (1569–1612)

The way of the world as it is,
What can I do about fleeting time?
As the last chrysanthemums shiver in late autumn,
Cricket chirps grow louder as night deepens.
The sad moon shines on the windows;
And passing winds rustle branches.
Recalling what has happened over the last ten years,
I sit before a lamp, counting the moths flying into it.

Untitled

Kwŏn P'il (1569–1612)

Now the riverbank is covered with the exuberant green.
One who has bid farewell can barely find his way.
He recalls the first embrace on a quiet spring night
When the plum blossoms wilted and a nightingale sadly sang.

On the Road

Kwŏn P'il (1569–1612)

As the sun sets, I step into a lone lodge
Whose brushwood gate remains open deep in the mountains.
At cockcrow, I inquire about the road ahead.
Yellow leaves rustle, flying into me.

At Song-gang's Grave

KWŎN P'IL (1569–1612)

In deserted mountains, rain drizzles on fallen leaves,
While a man of grace and great gusto lies in silence.
It grieves me that I cannot now offer you a drink;
Did the song you once sang foretell my sorrow this morning?

Chŏng Ch'ŏl, whose pen name was Song-gang, was the poet's teacher. He
wrote a famous drinking song in Korean, in which the *carpe diem* theme was
emphatically presented.

Kwŏn P'il declined all offers of public office, and spent his entire life devoted
to poetry and wine. Tried for a poem in which he satirized the royal family's
dissipation, he was found guilty and exiled. On his way to the place of exile,
many people gathered to offer him drink, whereupon he drank himself to
death.

Longing

CH'ŎNG-HAK (1570–1654)

Surrounding mountains and streams double my sorrow.
I turn my eyes to the sky's edge twelve times a day.
While the moon shines on the window of my solitary hut,
A wave of longing subsides, only to be followed by another.

Ch'ŏng-hak was a Buddhist monk.

To a Drunken Guest

YI MAE-CH'ANG (1573–1610)

Do not pull my sleeve, drunken man,
For my soft robe is easily torn.
Not that my silk is so precious;
Our tender feelings may also tear.

In Reply to a Seducer's Poem

Yi Mae-ch'ang (1573–1610)

Though ashamed of being an entertaining-woman,
I have always loved the moonlit plum blooming in
    the cold.
Others do not know my deeply hidden love for him;
Every passerby tries his hand at winning me.

Spring Rain

YI MAE-CH'ANG (1573–1610)

After seeing you off, I sadly close the gate.
Tears fall, staining my sleeve.
As I lie alone in this quiet, empty room,
Thin rain falls in the evening yard.

Longing

YI MAE-CH'ANG (1573–1610)

Last night, geese flew crying in the autumn frost;
Rising from sewing for my love, I climb the high pavilion.
From the front so far away, news cannot reach here;
Alone, I lean dizzy at the railing, while worries fill my heart.

Untitled

Yı Mae-ch'ang (1573–1610)

Moonlit bamboo shadows linger on the window.
Windblown peach blossoms drift in the air.
Alone, unable to sleep, I lean on the small railing –
A lotus picker sings far from the rivershore.

Valedictory Poem

YI MAE-CH'ANG (1573–1610)

The dusty world abounds in pain, surging like waves;
Many a weary, lonesome night I spent at my solitary home.
As dusk falls on the bridge, I turn to look back;
Cloud-covered mountains loom to block my view.

Yi Mae-ch'ang, a famous *kisaeng* of the mid-Chosŏn Dynasty, was an
accomplished poet, musician, and dancer. Many of her poems reveal her
longing for Yu Hi-kyŏng, whose works also appear in this volume.

A Woman's Complaint

CH'OE KI-NAM (16TH –17TH CENTURY)

I still keep the mirror you gave me,
And still remember the time you gave it.
Now you are gone, only the empty mirror remains.
What need have I to hold it up to darken my brows?

Ch'oe Ki-nam was a poet of the mid-Chosŏn Dynasty.

Holding the Receding Year

SON P'IL-TAE (1599-?)

I sit before the lamp in my cold room until dawn.
As the remaining hours get smaller, my heartache deepens.
It is as when I bade farewell to my love at sunset
On a day when I was still a loafer south of the river.

Son P'il-tae was a poet of the mid-Chosŏn Dynasty.

Mourning

YI KYE (1603–1642)

Half the dresses you brought to our wedding are still new;
My grief deepens as I open your closet and fold them.
What you have cherished all your life I send with you
To the empty mountain, where they will turn to dust.

Yi Kye, a courtier of the mid-Chosŏn Dynasty, was executed for treason.

Walking in the Mountains

KANG PAEK-NYŎN (1603–1681)

Walking in the mountains, I hear no human voice;
In the quiet mountains, spring birds sing.
Meeting a monk, I ask my way;
When he is gone, I am lost again.

Kang Paek-nyŏn was a courtier-scholar of the mid-Chosŏn Dynasty whose
remarkable political career lasted nearly fifty years.

To My Wife

O DAL-JE (1609–1637)

Though our conjugal love still deepens,
Our happiness lasted less than two years.
Now we are ten thousand miles from each other,
Our pledge of a hundred years together has proved vain.
The width of the land is hard for a letter to cross;
The breadth of the sky delays my journey even in dreams.
Now I cannot be sure of my safe return,
I bid you to raise well our unborn child.

O Dal-je, a courtier of the mid-Chosŏn Dynasty, strongly opposed making a humiliating truce with the invading Ching army. When the war ended, he was taken to China, along with two other opponents of the truce, and was executed there.

Watching a Crow Feeding Its Mother

PAK CHANG-WŎN (1612–1671)

Though I am blessed in that my parents still live,
Poverty forbids me to offer them good food.
While the wretched bird moves an onlooker's heart,
I can only shed tears, watching it feed its mother.

Pak Chang-wŏn was an official of the mid-Chosŏn Dynasty.

Longing for Home

YI TAE-SŎ (17TH CENTURY)

My heart aches to recall the moon above Mount Ami;
My heart aches to recall the clouds around Mount Ami.
Though clouds follow the moon wherever I go,
It is the crystal-clear peak of Mount Ami that I long for.

Passing Hwanggan

PAK CH'I-WŎN (1680–1764)

My legs feel weak already, when the day is long;
Wine warmed on the spring stove flows green.
Spring haze rises along shafts of sunlight;
Ducks, refreshed in cold water, fly above the stream.
I cut reeds for soles on my worn straw shoes,
And tell my boy again not to take the wrong road.
I ask a passing monk which way is he going;
Smiling, he points to thin clouds floating over the peaks.

Pak Ch'i-wŏn was an influential courtier during the reign of King Yŏngjo.

Sunset

PAK MUN-SU (1691–1756)

The setting sun, pouring out red, hangs upon the green hill;
A cold-stricken crow flies to fade into white clouds.
The traveler inquiring about the ferry whips his horse in haste;
The monk returning to his temple in a hurry carries his staff.
The cow grazing in the field casts its long shadow;
The woman awaiting her man lowers her head in worry.
On the road across the stream where an old fog-encircled tree
      stands,
The short-haired woodcutter returns home, playing his flute.

Pak Mun-su, a courtier and man at arms, is known to have been an expert in
military affairs. Many tales of his feats as an *osa*, a clandestine inspector of the
provincial government dispatched by the king, still survive.

Watching Wine-Filtering

NAM YU-YONG (1698-1773)

Watching my wife filter wine while my child holds a jar,
I sit, propping my chin, enjoying its aroma.
Last year a single measure of rice yielded three bottles;
This year, it is ten cups less.
I say, if good wine can make one drunk faster,
So what if I get ten cups less?
Don't hesitate, woman, wondering if it's good;
Hand me a bottle first, so I may taste.

Nam Yu-yong was a high-ranking government official of the mid-Chosŏn
Dynasty

At My Brother's Grave

CHO JAE-HO (1702–1762)

The old house is kept by his wife and children
While the years pass this empty mountain.
Though grief deepens, remaining tears dry up;
Loneliness pierces one who has lost the other half.
As I stare out where bleak clouds end,
Far-off wild geese call to surprise me.
Now I have lost one blessing in life,
I pity myself, who will die alone.

Cho Jae-ho was a prominent courtier in the reign of King Yŏngjo.

Upon Returning Home

SHIN KWANG-SU (1712–1775)

After a half-year's sojourn in the royal town,
I return home to face what I have not known before.
As always, my children greet me at the gate;
But the one who would rise from the spindle is no more.
Painfully I recall how we lived in poverty;
A heartless creature, she left this world before me.
Before the empty curtain, I cry out in grief
While loneliness pierces deep through my aging body.

Shin Kwang-su was a government official.

At a Cemetery of the KISAENGS

YI DŎK-MU (1741–1793)

Grass on the mounds is green, as if it were their silk,
While the scent of their perfume lingers around their dark rooms.
You, who are now in full bloom, don't be proud:
Here lie countless beauties who were once like you.

Yi Dŏk-mu was a great intellectual who believed in the importance of practical
learning.

Mu-gye Ravine

KO HU-YŎL (CIRCA 1750–1800)

Morning sunrays through trees dispel night fog.
After the rain, streams rush over the rocks.
Now old, I have returned after ten long years:
White clouds float as always above the dark ravine.

Ko Hu-yŏl was a poet of the late Chosŏn Dynasty.

To My Love

SOHONG (DATE UNKNOWN)

When north winds blow snow against my window,
I lie sleepless through the long weary night.
If no one visits my grave on a day years hence,
How pitiful am I, though I bloom like a flower today.

Sohong was probably a *kisaeng*.

Tears of Farewell

TOHWA (DATE UNKNOWN)

I first met you on the Naktong River;
Today I bid farewell at Pojewon gate.
Though fallen peach blossoms leave no flowery trace,
How can I not remember you when the moon shines bright?

The person who wrote this poem was a *kisaeng* named Tohwa, the literal
meaning of which is "peach blossoms."

Wilting of the Flowers

ANONYMOUS BARMAID
(19TH CENTURY)

Only last night I slept near blooming flowers.
This morning I crossed a stream where fallen petals drift.
Life is like the spring that no sooner comes than goes:
I had hardly seen flowers bloom when I saw them wilt.

To My Faraway Love

KYEHYANG (19TH CENTURY)

Separated by cloud-covered mountains,
I can be happy, laughing near you, only in my dreams.
I wake to see your deserted pillow beside mine;
I turn to the dim lamp, cold light on my face.
When shall I rejoice to see your face again?
I suffer now in vain, my heart an ache.
Outside the window, rain drips on paulownia leaves again,
While my longing draws another stream of tears.

Kyehyang was a concubine.

Waiting for My Love

NUNG-UN (19TH CENTURY)

My love said he would come at moonrise;
The moon has risen, but he has not come.
I presume that where my love lives
The mountain is so high the moon rises slowly.

Nung-un was probably a mistress or a concubine.

Autumn Rain

HYEJŎNG (DATE UNKNOWN)

Mount Kŭmgang stands in September windswept rain,
While every single rainy leaf mourns autumn.
For the last ten years I have shed silent tears;
Only my tear-soaked robe knows my grief.

Hyejŏng was a female Buddhist monk.

Upon Joining the Garrison

CHO SU-SAM (1762–1849)

Though I harbored ambition in my youthful days,
I have not accomplished any martial feat till now.
An urgent post calling for men at arms
Made me ride a stallion to this front.
On my belt, a sky-piercing sword;
In my heart, lines worthy of being carved in stone.
When a thousand years have gone,
Who will recall the name of Captain Cho?

Cho Su-sam was a poet of the late Chosŏn Dynasty.

The Martial Post

YI HI-BAL (1768–1849)

As dusk falls on the frontier castle, I lean alone on the railing.
The tune of the enemy's pipe floats over the towers.
I ask, "Where is the line separating us from China?"
Smiling, you point beyond the river where a mountain looms.

Yi Hi-bal was a Minister of National Defense during the late
Chosŏn Dynasty.

The Nightingale

SHIN WI (1769–1847)

Pear blossoms bloom through the moonlit night;
A blood-choked nightingale breaks the silence.
Knowing that pathos breeds only pain in the heart,
Though free of wordly concern, I am still unable to sleep.

Chrysanthemums

SHIN WI (1769–1847)

Sharing wine with a visitor is a pleasure,
But I do not mind drinking alone.
Fearing the chrysanthemums laugh at my empty bottle,
I send my books and coat to ensure paying later.

Shin Wi was a poet, calligrapher, and courtier of the late Chosŏn Dynasty.

Fallen Leaves Around a Stone Well

HONG KIL-JU (1786–1841)

I like to sit in the shade of the exuberant elm.
It surpasses flowers in grace and beauty.
You'd better not sweep, lingering around the well;
Let autumn leaves fall to cover the ground.

Hong Kil-ju was a scholar of the late Chosŏn Dynasty.

A Widow's Grief

CHŎNG SANG-KWAN

(18TH–19TH CENTURY)

On the festive day of the Full Moon of Autumn
A widow weeps all day before a mound on the hill.
Down in the valley, the rice has turned gold;
What she planted with her man, she now must eat alone.

Chŏng Sang-kwan was a poet of the late Chosŏn Dynasty.

The Full-Moon Hill

YI KYŎNG-MIN (1814–1883)

Now five hundred years of kingly glory is gone,
Its pomp has left no trace but exuberant pines.
Upon ruins where flowers have wilted, sadness reigns;
The nightingale's song deepens pathos over castle grounds.
Plowed fields encroach the palace stairs;
Spring grass, undeterred, grows over the railings.
Though it grieves my heart to watch it,
Kingdoms rise and fall like a flowing stream.

Yi Kyŏng-min was a scholar toward the end of the Chosŏn Dynasty.

On the Ruins of a Palace

NAM BYŎNG-CH'OL (1817–1863)

To the ruins of a palace buried in silence
Autumn comes to dress trees in red.
While the west wind blows on royal tombs,
Mountains and rivers bathe in evening light.
As listless tears well in my eyes, I wonder
Whether their age-long worship of Buddha did them any good.
Grief and anger become inherited sentiments;
Many a loyal subject filled the rooms in vain.

Nam Byŏng-ch'ol was a courtier and scientist toward the end of the Chosŏn
Dynasty.

Drinking Alone on a Spring Night

AN JUNG-SŎP (19TH CENTURY)

Having indulged in a spring dream, I sober up at dawn –
To see the bright moon above a branch of plum blossom.
At last I've made up my mind to lead a simple, carefree life:
I'd rather buy a set of classics than fertile patches of land.

Ahn Jung-sŏp was a man of letters toward the end of the Chosŏn Dynasty.

Listening to the Wild Geese

KANG WI (1820–1884)

What need for them to worry about livelihood?
If autumn comes or spring goes, should they get busy?
Their only pleasure is to remain carefree in the cold air;
They seldom descend to mud, staying above the clouds.

Kang Wi, a scholar-poet toward the end of the Chosŏn Dynasty, was the
publisher of the first newspaper in Korea.

The Moonlit Pond

YI GŎN-CH'ANG (1852–1898)

Unable to sleep because of the full moon,
I step out of my cottage and walk to the pond.
Lotus flowers have all shed their petals,
Yet their fragrance still lingers.
A soft breeze lifts the lotus leaves;
Deep in the water a star glitters.
I dip my hand in the pond to catch it.
The chill of the water pierces to my bones.

Yi Gŏn-ch'ang was a scholar-poet toward the end of the Chosŏn Dynasty. He
was a great friend of Hwang Hyŏn, whose poems also appear in this volume.

Seeing Yŏng-jae in Dreams

HWANG HYŎN (1855–1910)

What pains me most on earth
Is to see my friend only in dreams;
Joy lasts only for a moment;
I wake to my long grief again.
Wind blows and bamboo rustles;
Snow casts light on the empty window.
I put on my clothes and step out alone:
Cold sky studded with countless stars.

"Yŏng-jae" in the title of the poem is Yi Gŏn-ch'ang, whose poem "The Moonlit Pond" appears in this volume.

At the Grave of Yŏng-jae

HWANG HYŎN (1855–1910)

Though grief remains fresh after twelve long years,
The mound already crumbles on the autumn mountain.
Pursuing the right path, you did not seek comfort;
Even now you could not have forsaken your love of learning.
In the clear distant sky, wild geese are flocking;
Still farther, hazy clouds spread wide.
Do not grieve over lying here alone:
Even when alive, did you not prefer to avoid the crowd?

New Year's Eve

Hwang Hyŏn (1855–1910)

I wake up to face the onslaught of sad thoughts;
The chilly-looking lamp doesn't draw me near.
As I try to hold the receding year before the gong sounds,
An aging man's face looms in the mirror.
Unable to sleep, I toss about in bed,
And console myself, humming verses.
Warbling softly, flowing beneath the snow,
The rivulet already knows that spring is coming.

On Spring Commemoration Day

HWANG HYŎN (1855–1910)

This year again, Spring Commemoration Day has come;
I turn my eyes to grave mounds in the mountains.
Weary of wandering the troubled world, I see flowers bloom;
Forcing a smile in the breeze, I lift a wine cup.
Walking in thin rain, I let my face be drenched;
Before my eyes a clear stream cleansing me of pathos.
A mere recluse with his books is of no use, after all:
Last night, an urgent letter came, calling for men at arms.

Upon Returning to My Birthplace

HWANG HYŎN (1855–1910)

Ten days are gone already since I left home;
I wonder if the scenery remains the same.
Though trees in the field fade into distance,
Autumn light overflows thick chrysanthemums.
The tall castle casts its shadow in the cold;
A clear stream ripples in late dusk.
Sad, seeing geese flying south,
That have to pass by once, year after year.

Regret for the Spring Receding

HWANG HYŎN (1855–1910)

As peach blossom fragrance fades and green deepens,
Weary bees buzz over clay-built fences.
The warbling rivulet is no longer dear to me:
It carries away petals fallen from the breeze.

An Abortive Visit

HWANG HYŎN (1855–1910)

What if I fall asleep alone tonight?
The moon hidden in trees casts only half its light.
When I thought there was a man outside,
It was only the wind, rattling bamboo.

Putting an End to Myself (1)

HWANG HYŎN (1855–1910)

Choked by venomous air, the kingly star has moved;
In the dark palace, time wears on, slow and weary.
The King's command, hereafter, will not shake the land again;
On this sheet bearing a poem, many a streak of tears.

Putting an End to Myself (2)

HWANG HYŎN (1855–1910)

Birds and beasts mourn, while the whole earth frowns,
For this land is now drowned in shame.
By autumn lamp I close the book to think of my country's fate;
What a burden to be a man who has read enough to know!

Hwang Hyŏn was an historian and poet toward the end of the Chosŏn
Dynasty. The two previous poems are from a group of four that he wrote on
the night he committed suicide, upon hearing that Korea had been annexed
to Japan by a treaty in 1910.

A Night at Ch'ŏn-un Temple

YI BYŎNG-HO (1870–1943)

As the moon comes out to fill the dewy sky,
Guests find it hard to sleep deeply in the temple.
Thick rushes resound in the vale of peonies;
Wind at dawn blows over paulownia leaves.
Though my lines may still shake the world, my body wanes;
But there will be time for the growing splendor of mountains.
Now we are granted poetic indulgence in a temple room,
Buddha will not frown at us while we spend a noisy night.

Chang-an Temple of Mount Kŭmgang

YI BYŎNG-HO (1870–1943)

Unearthly scenery of the hermits' world unfolds;
The dark stream, circling white rocks, flows on.
The world-embracing light of Buddha shines.
Who recalls the glory and shame of the world of dust?
The sky pours on the cliff a thousand-foot waterfall,
And the clear stream washes away deep-layered dust.
As I bid reluctant farewell to leave for the far south,
April flowers bloom on trees soaked in spring.

Nine-Dragon Falls

Yi Byŏng-ho (1870–1943)

When the chill of the waterfall makes it feel like autumn,
Its column sends up the high arch of a rainbow.
The deep pond is crystal-clear to the rocky floor;
The Milky Way pours down from the head of the clouds.
The blue mountain trembles in foggy rain hiding its color,
And in bright sunrays, deafening thunder resounds.
They say nine dragons reside in that cave;
An abyss of dark water makes an onlooker shudder.

On the Piro Peak

YI BYŎNG-HO (1870–1943)

As I turn east on Piro Peak, the sea stretches endlessly.
Where can immobile continents find a spot to link them?
Soaring high for countless ages far above the dusty world,
Innumerable peaks, bowing or retreating, pay homage to the sky.
Though shaped like Buddha, they are rocks, after all;
As I look east to sunrise, fog blocks my view.
I laugh at my small self dwindled into a mustard seed:
I sigh deeply in the howling wind, while all my thoughts disappear.

Mount Kŭmgang on the Sea

YI BYŎNG-HO (1870–1943)

Heaven has raised Mount Kŭmgang both on land and sea;
Sea and mountain share one spirit, unseen by the world.
While shadows of rising and sinking rocks linger on the sails,
The mirror-like sea reflects their many shapes and poses.
Night chill threatens snow and frost with the rising mist;
The moon brightens, shining on cranes floating among clouds.
Now mirage and winding mist have fully revealed themselves,
The unfathomable skill of the Creator must have reached its depth.

Yi Byŏng-ho was a student of Hwang Hyŏn. A renowned poet in his time, he
served as the head judge for numerous poetry contests.

鳴戲衣鳴海岳嘶樵壺世

勞也況淪秋鐙擁卷恨千古

誰作人品戲字人

曾無志厦半堵功足垂成仁

不是忠止竟借能追尹穀

當時愧不歸陳東

亂離滾到白頭年　幾合捐生却未然
今日真成無可奈　輝輝風燭照蒼天

妖氛晻翳帝星移　九闕沉沉晝漏遲
詔勅從今無復有　琳琅一紙淚千絲

("Putting an End to Myself," Hwang Hyŏn)

Index of Authors' Names

Index of Titles

About the Translator

BORN IN SEOUL, in 1943, Sung-Il Lee grew up in Korea and did his undergraduate studies in English at Yonsei University, Seoul. After fulfilling his military service, he went to the United States for graduate studies in English. Having completed his graduate work (MA, University of California at Davis, 1973; PHD, Texas Tech University, 1980), he returned to Korea to teach at his *alma mater*.

Twice a *Korean Times* translation prize-winner, Sung-Il Lee has taught Korean literature at the University of Toronto and at the University of Washington. His first book of translations, *The Wind and the Waves* (Asian Humanities Press, Berkeley), won the 1990 Grand Prize in the Republic of Korea Literary Awards. He currently serves as the Director of the Institute of Translation at Yonsei University.

Book design & composition by John D. Berry Design, using Adobe Page-Maker 6.0 on a Macintosh iivx and PageMaker 6.5 on a Power 120. The typeface is Minion multiple master, designed by Robert Slimbach as part of the Adobe Originals type library. Minion is based on typefaces of the later Renaissance, but is derived from no single source. Slimbach designed Minion in 1990, then expanded it in 1992 to become a multiple master font – the first to include a size axis for optical scaling. *Printed by Bang Printing.*